Table of Contents

How to use this book:

It is recommended that this workbook be completed in order, as many of the skills build on each other. To reference specific areas of learning, use the Index at the back of this book.

Colors includes guided coloring activities and opportunities to practice color identification and matching. The activities also improve language and math skills.

Sort and Match includes activities for sorting and matching things that are alike, identifying things that belong in the same group, and matching a part to its whole. Activities for recognizing sizes, colors, numbers, letters and patterns are also included.

Sizes and Shapes focuses on identifying and drawing basic shapes. Identifying sizes, lengths and heights are also reinforced. Extending shape patterns improves skills in beginning math and visual discrimination.

Letters activities are designed to teach children how to recognize capital and lowercase letters of the alphabet at the beginning of words and within words. Children also gain practice forming the letters according to an approved standardized educational method of manuscript writing. Visual discrimination skills are also sharpened.

Beginning Letter Sounds includes activities that help children identify letter sounds at the beginning of words. Recognizing capital and lowercase letter partners is also taught and reinforced.

Word Families activities focus on common word families and rhyme. Exercises reinforce both phonics and spelling skills.

This book also includes interactive learning tools. The decoder is used on pages 53-78, 110-131, and 135-160. Your child can use it to check his or her answers once he/she has completed an activity. Cut-out flash cards are provided for the letters of the alphabet on pages 79-84.

Colors

Teach your child to:
- identify and name colors
- sort and match colors
- recognize and continue color patterns
- improve skills in visual discrimination
- improve language and numerical skills

Blue has lost her color! Can you help Blue color the items? Great!

Blue's going on a Color Camping Trip, and you're invited! So grab your backpack and let's get started. Color Blue's backpack your favorite color.

Blue is packing for her camping trip.
Will you help find her red flashlight? Circle it.
What other red things can you find?

Color these things red.

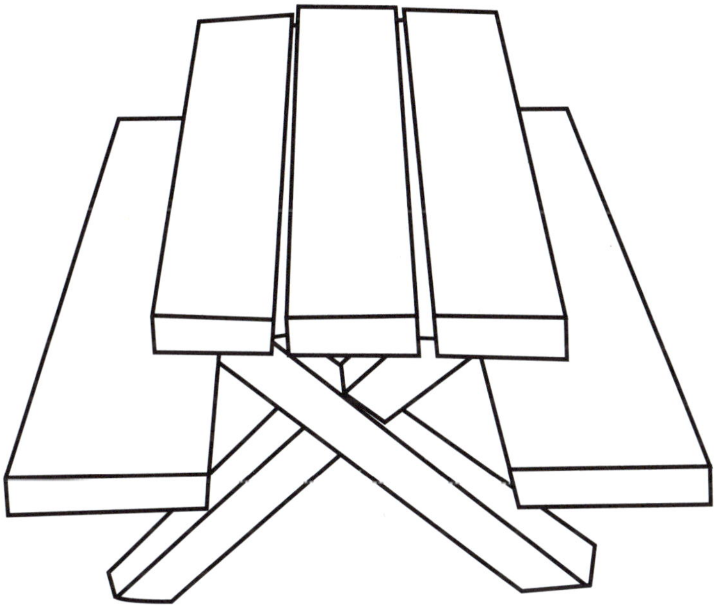

Look! Blue has a yellow map.
She can use it to find her way to the campsite. Will you help her? Great!
Draw a yellow line from Blue's house to the camp.

Circle the things that are yellow.

Blue made it to the campsite. Her friends are here, too! Will you color the water blue? Color Periwinkle's hat blue, too.

What else can you find at the lake?
Color the spaces with a • blue to see.

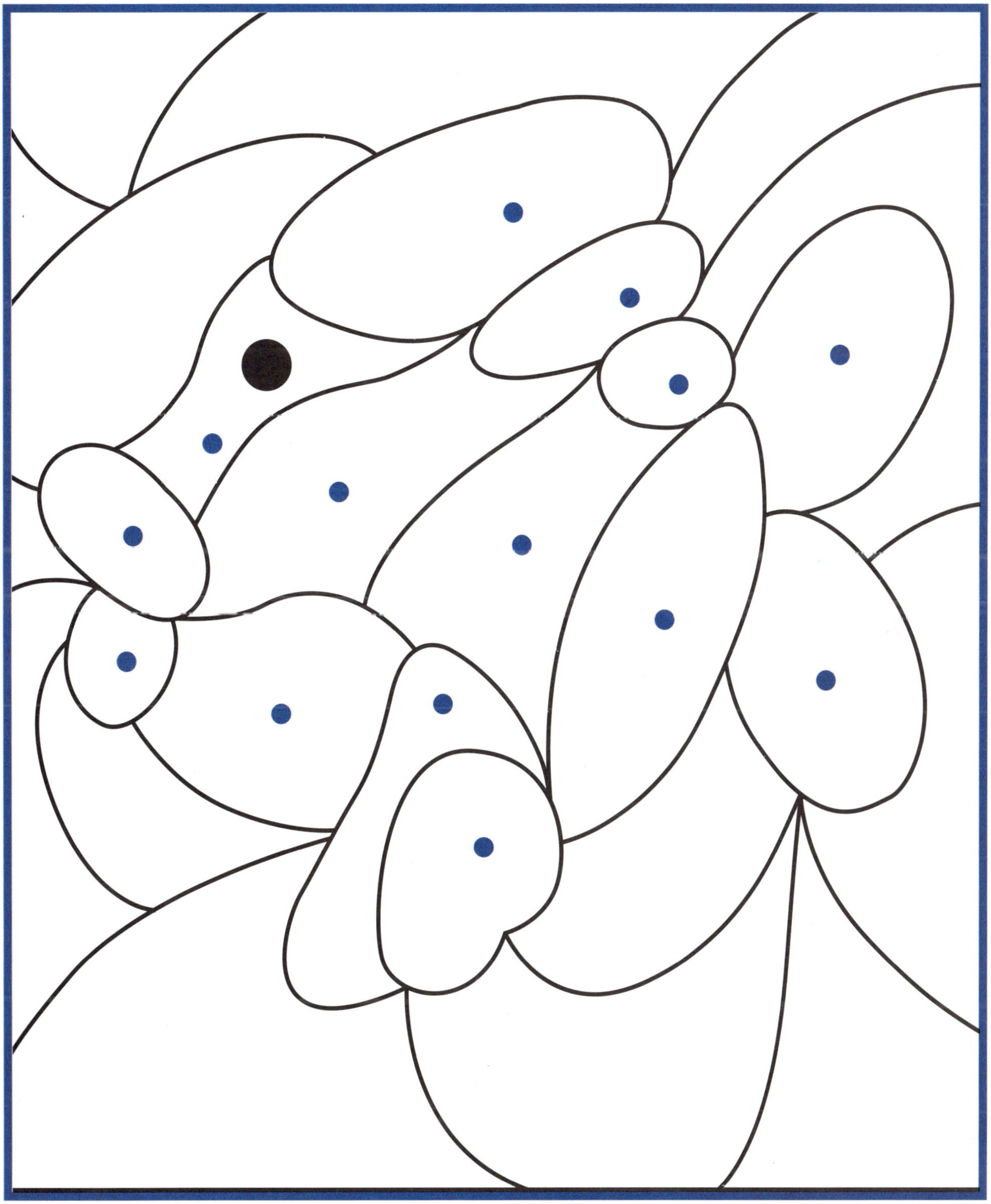

Blue and Green Puppy are going on a hike. They see many green things on their walk, like the grass on the ground. What else should be green? Color them!

What do you see that is green? Circle them.

Blue sees lots of animals on her hike. Will you draw a line from each animal to the matching color?

yellow

green

red

blue

Good job! Can you name each animal?

Continue the color patterns.

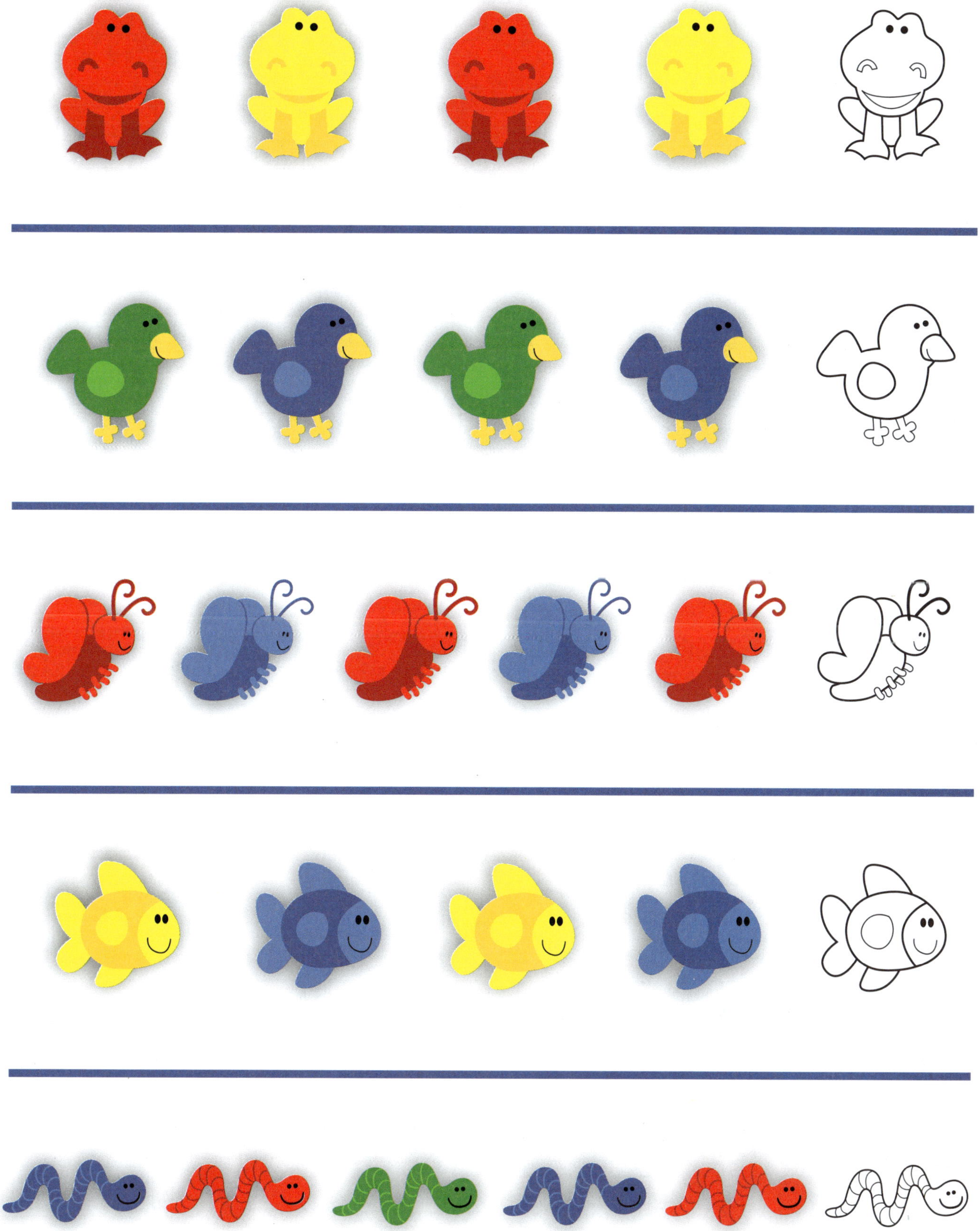

Magenta wants to go canoeing. She needs to wear something that will keep her safe. Connect the dots from **1** to **15** to find out what it is.

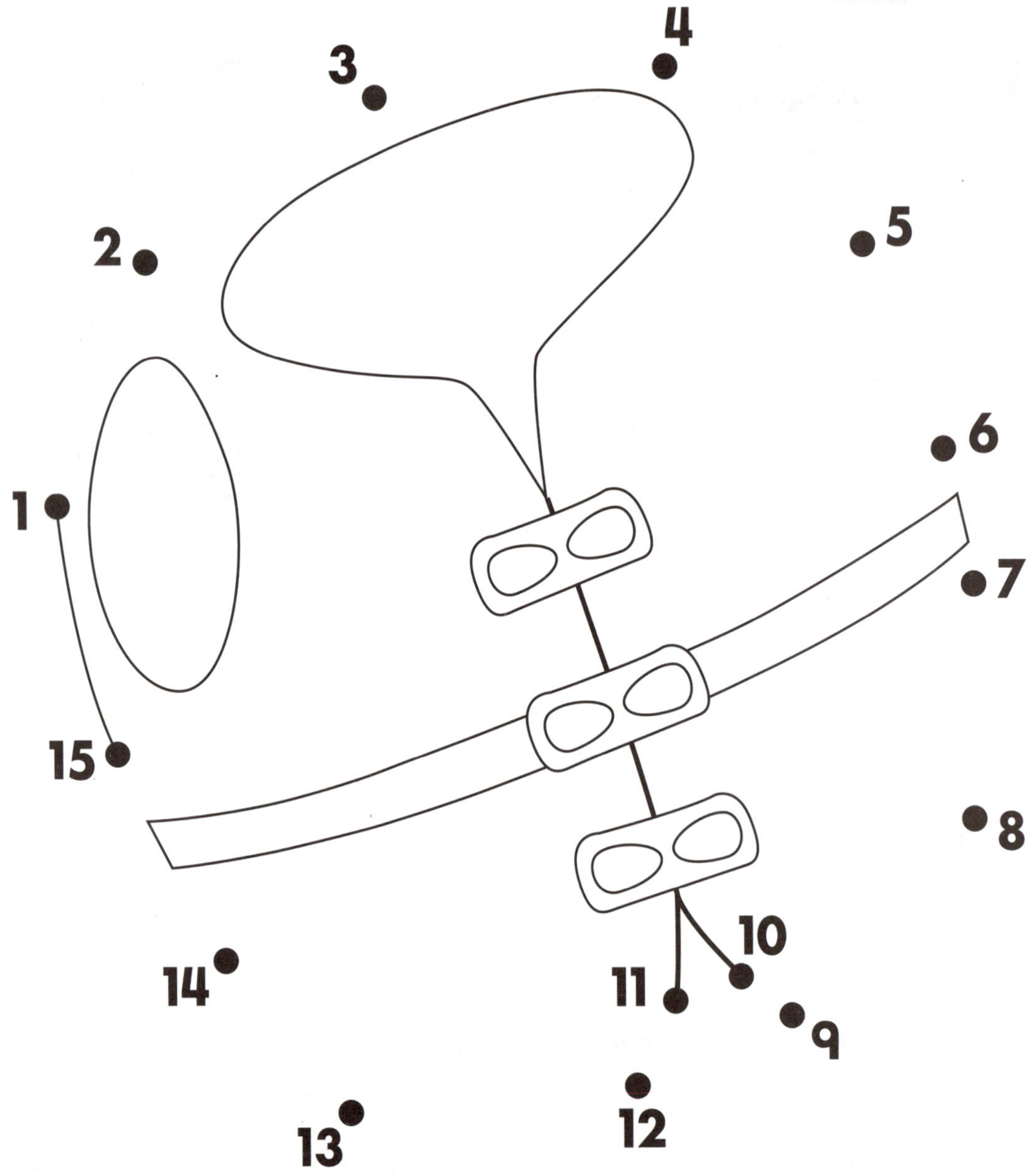

Good work! Now color it orange.

How many orange things do you see? Circle them.

Blue and Purple Kangaroo want to go sailing. Color the spaces with a ● purple to help them find a boat.

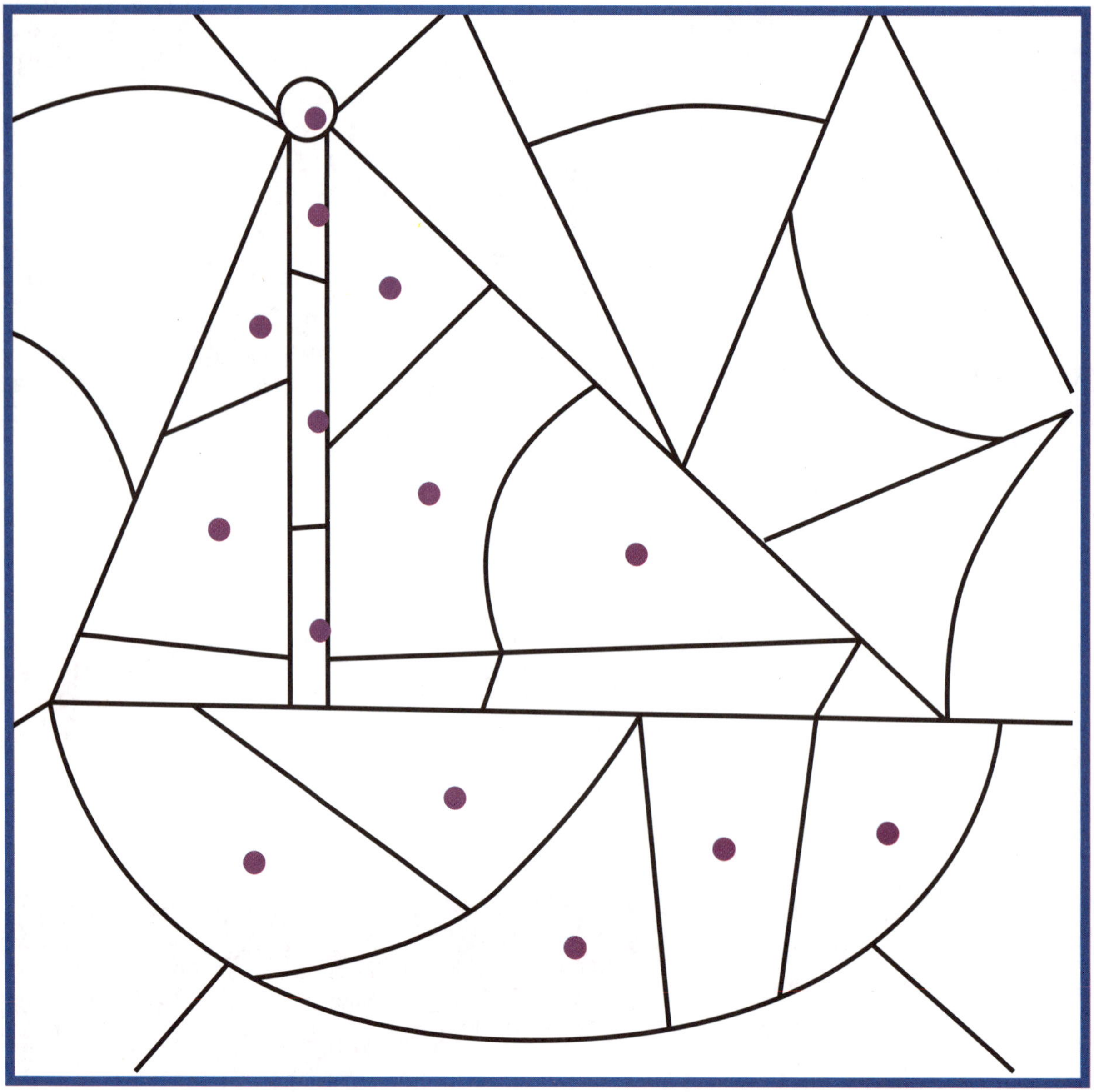

How many purple fish do you see?
Count and circle them.

Way to go! Now count the other fish.
What colors are they?

Blue sees a cabin in the woods. The cabin is brown.
What else do you see that is brown? Circle them!

Color these animals **brown.**

The sky is black at nighttime. That's when Blue goes to sleep. Do you know an animal that likes to fly around during the night? Connect the dots from 1 to 20 to find out.

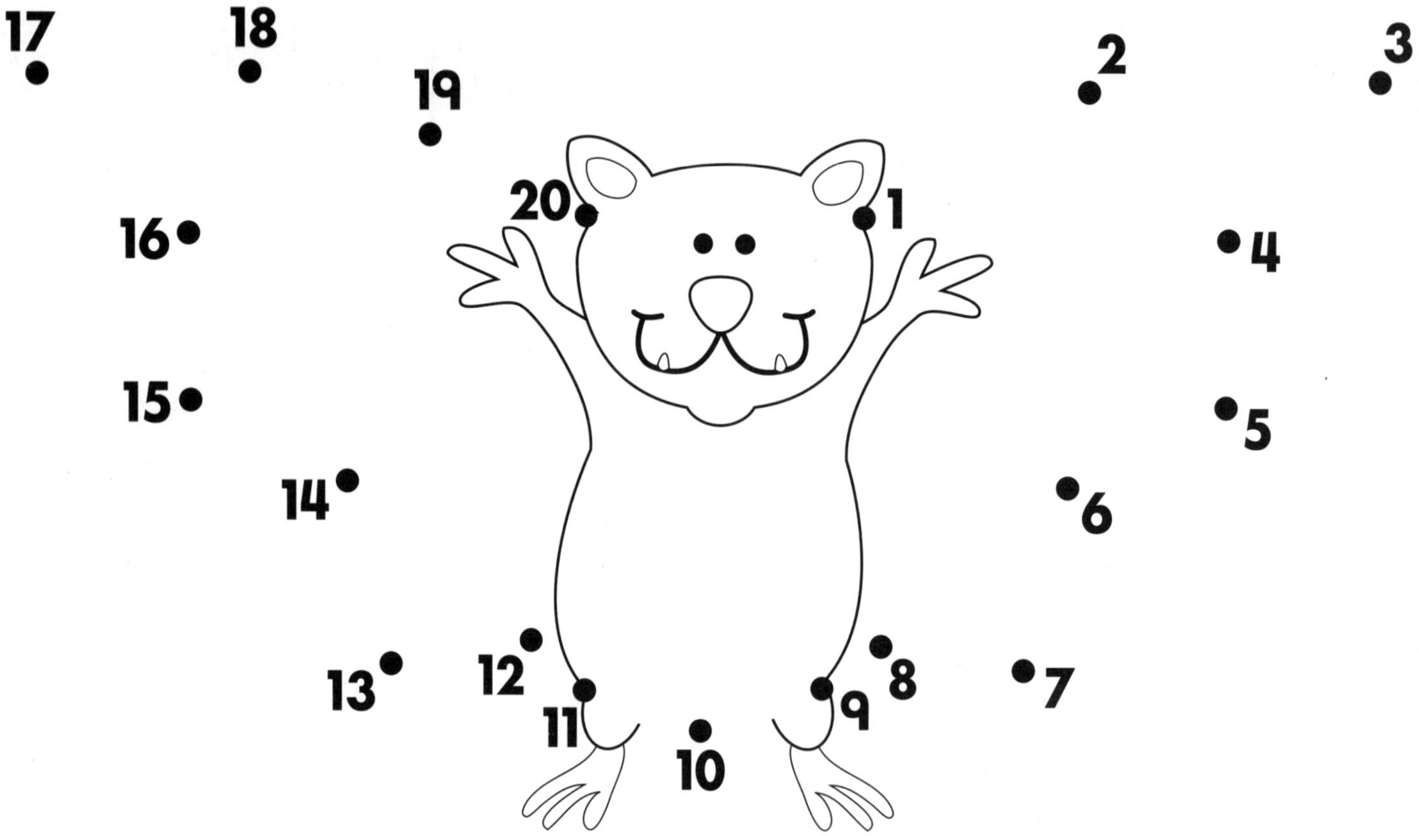

Good job! Color the animal black.

Circle the things that are black.

It's morning! Time for Blue to go home. Draw a line from Blue to her home to help her find her way.

Match each animal to the footprints that are the same color.

Blue and her friends had such a great time on their colorful camping trip. Thanks for helping! Color the picture using the code to see the different colors that they found.

1 = yellow
3 = green
5 = brown
7 = orange
2 = red
4 = blue
6 = black
8 = purple

Now draw and color your favorite thing about camping.

Colors are everywhere! Color the last book to continue the patterns.

Hey there! Now Blue and her friends are practicing their shapes. Do you want to practice, too? Great! Look! Blue drew a **square**. Now it's your turn!

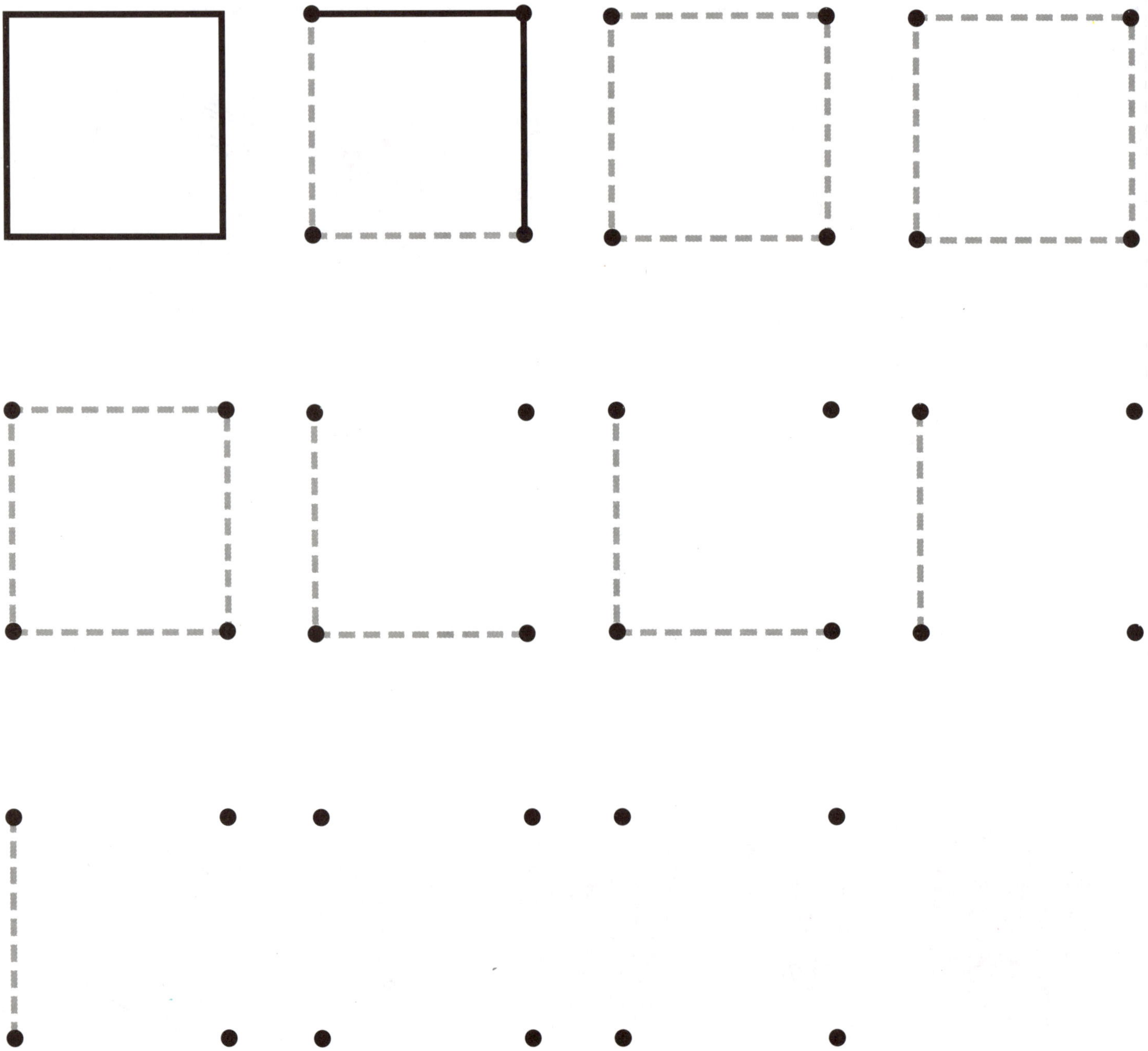

Will you help Mr. Salt and Mrs. Pepper trace around the snacks that are shaped like **squares**?

Periwinkle has big squares and little squares. Look at the patterns he made.

Draw and color 1 shape in each row to continue the patterns.

Magenta is drawing **circles**. Will you help her practice?

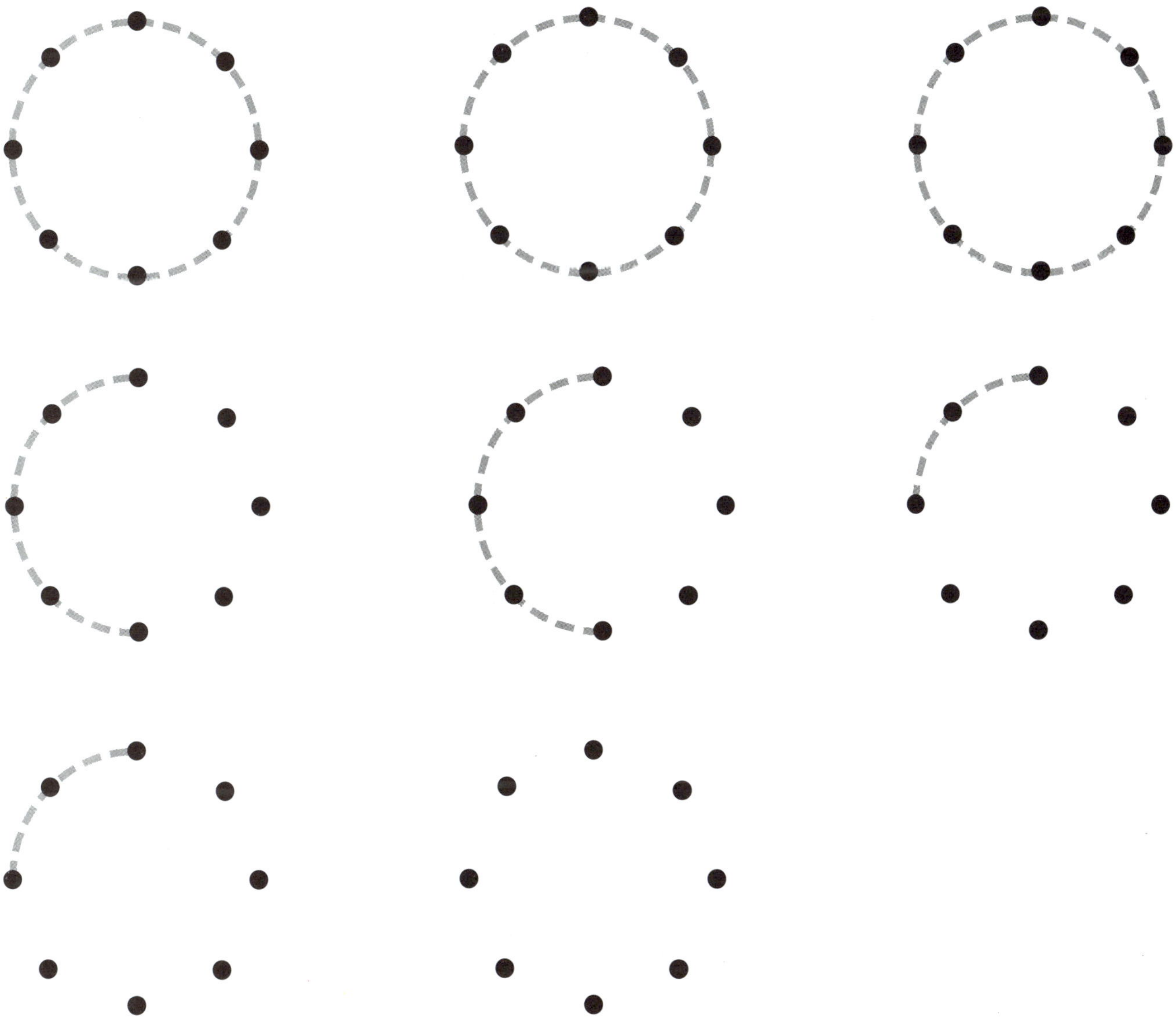

Trace the toys that are shaped like **circles**.

Green Puppy is making patterns with circles and squares. Will you help him continue the patterns? Great!

Draw and color 1 more shape in each row to continue the pattern.

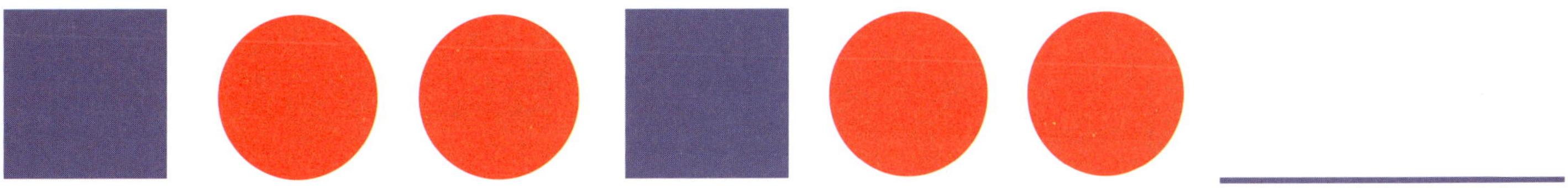

Slippery is shaped like a **rectangle**, so he drew a **rectangle**. Now it's your turn!

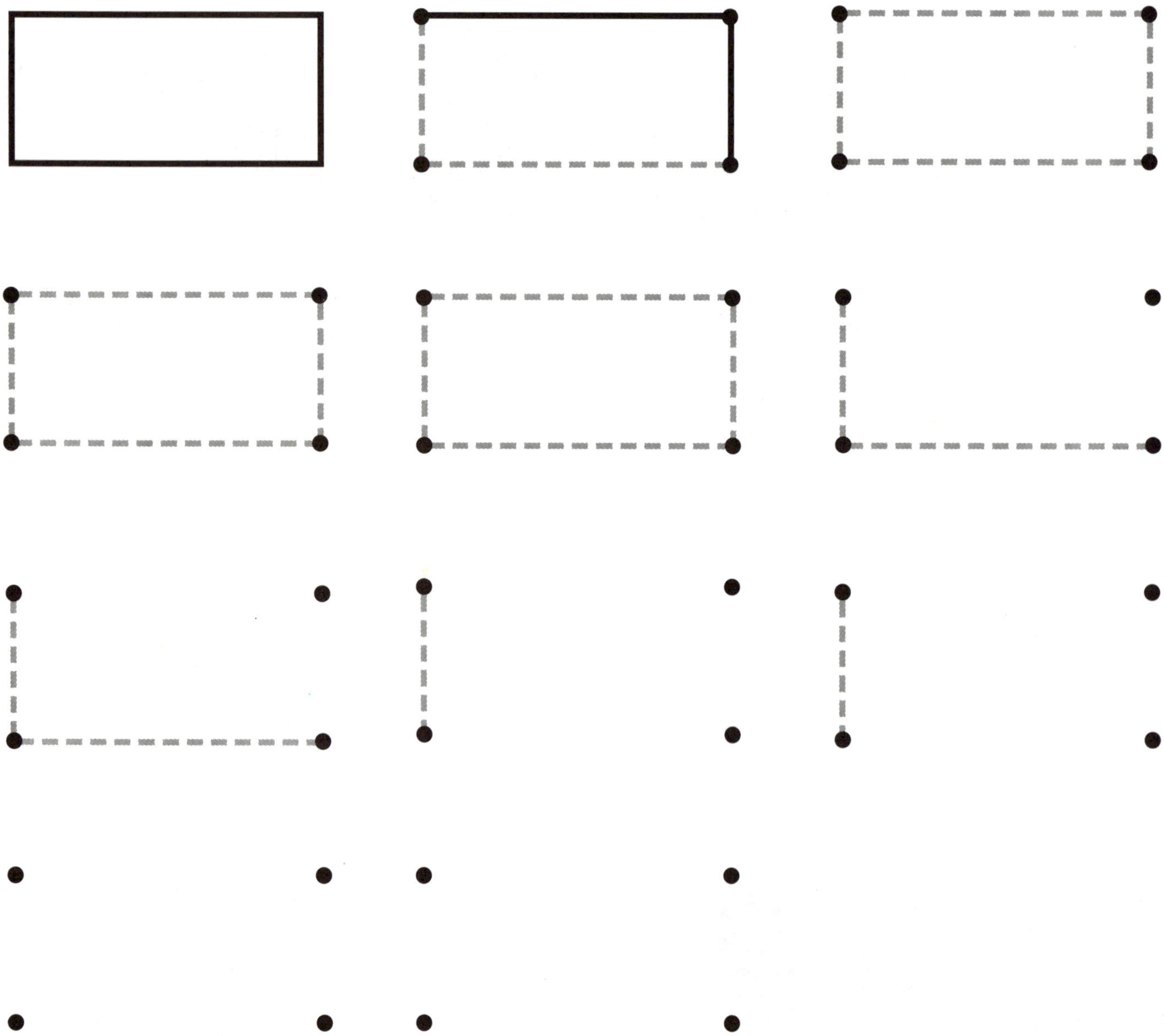

Which of Blue's things are shaped like **rectangles**? Trace them.

Mailbox loves Mail Time! Look how he made patterns with envelopes shaped like **rectangles** and **squares**.

Draw and color 1 more envelope in each row to continue the pattern.

Help Periwinkle draw **triangles**.

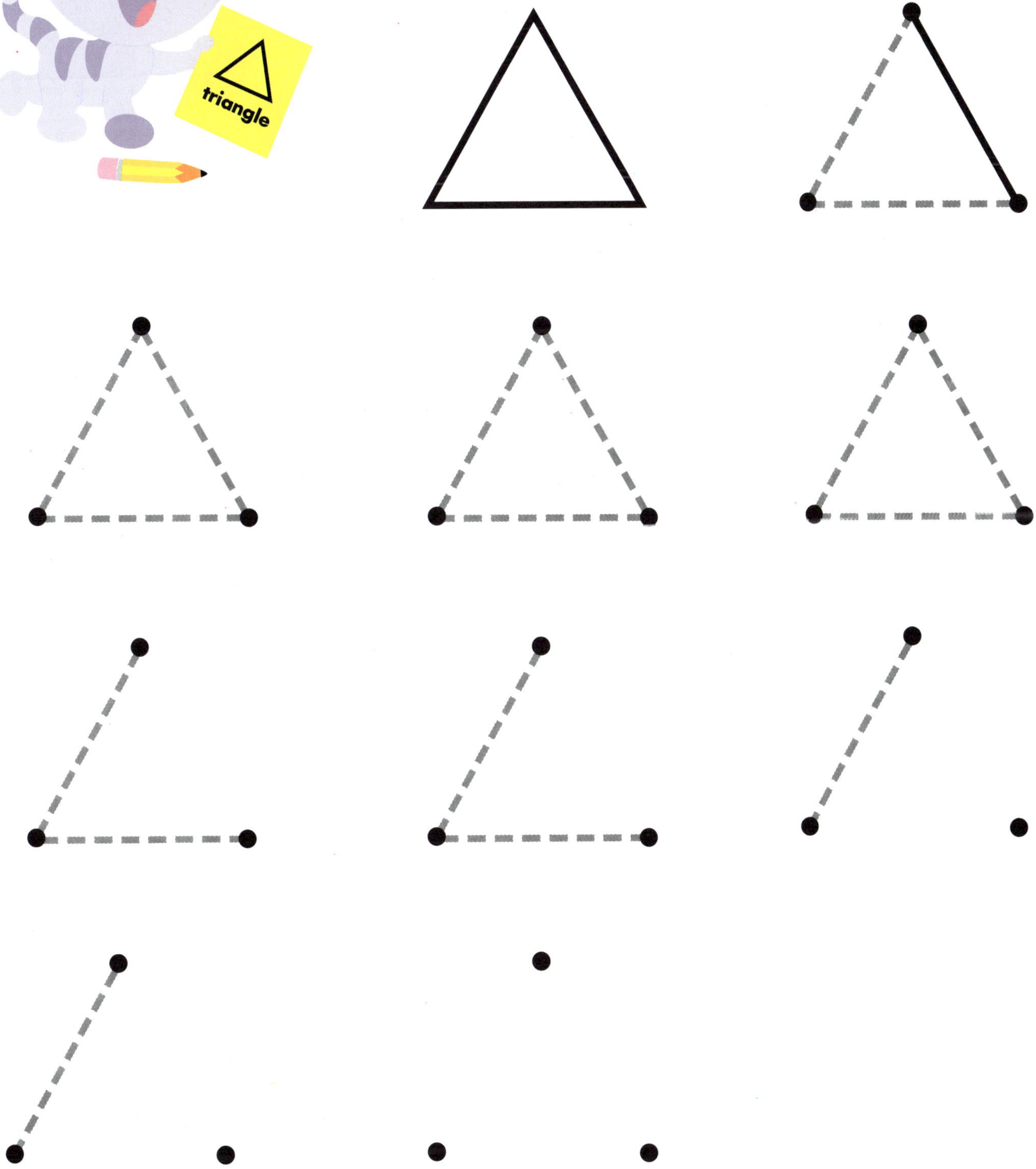

Trace the snacks that have a **triangle** shape.

Help Blue make patterns with triangles and circles.

Draw and color the next shape in each row.

Look! Orange Kitten drew an **oval**. Will you help her practice drawing more? Great!

Will you help Shovel and Pail find the things in the garden that have an **oval** shape? Trace them.

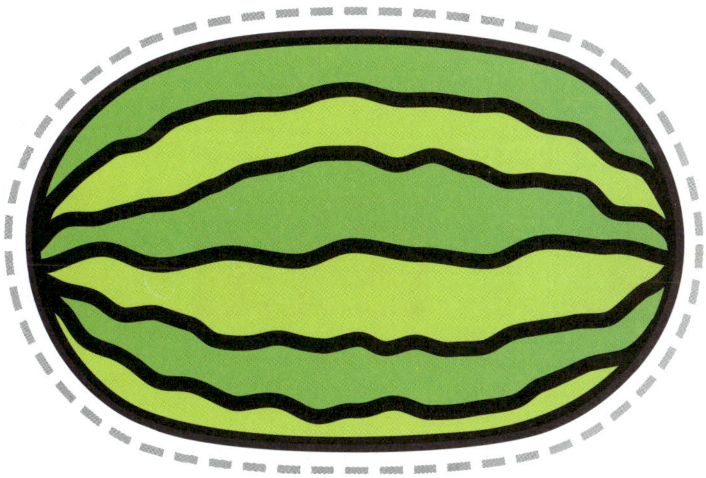

Green Puppy is making patterns with **ovals** and **rectangles**.

Draw and color 1 more shape in each row to help him continue the pattern.

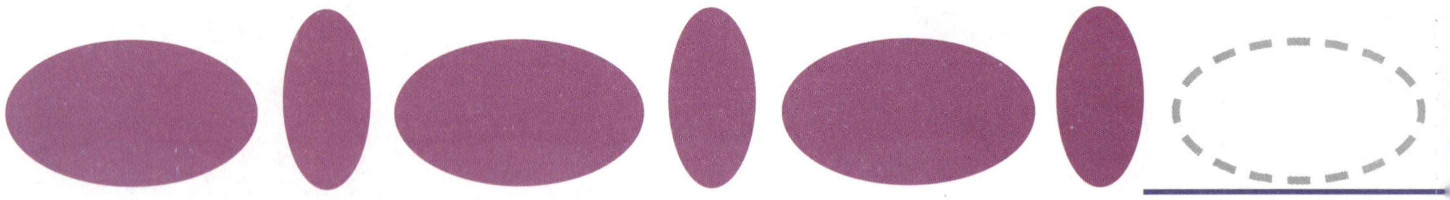

Purple Kangaroo drew a diamond.
Help him draw more.

Magenta loves to fly kites.
Trace the kites that are shaped like **diamonds**.

Help Orange Kitten make patterns with diamonds and triangles.

Draw and color the next shape in each row.

Blue loves you, so she drew a **heart**. Now it's your turn!

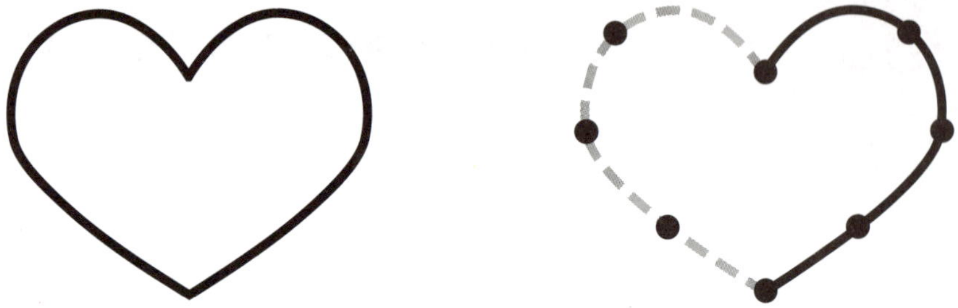

Some of Periwinkle's blocks have heart shapes. Trace all the hearts.

Look at the **star** Slippery drew!
Help him draw some more **stars**.

Magenta drew patterns with **stars** and **diamonds**. Now it's your turn!

Draw and color 1 more shape in each row to continue the pattern.

How many shapes can you find in this picture?
Trace them, then color the picture.
What do all the shapes make together?

Nice job! You're a great shape drawer!

Reveals hidden answers!

Includes a SPECIAL DECODER!

Decoder Workbook

Letters

Teach your child to:

- learn to write capital and lowercase letters
- recognize and name letters
- find letters in words and pictures
- develop pre-reading skills
- identify the letter sound

Write the letters that you know.

Write your name.

Find the letters that are hidden in the picture. Circle each one you find!

Blue is looking for letters of the alphabet today! Do you want to look too? Great! We can skidoo to Alphabet Town to look for the letters! You'll need the special decoder wand included in this book to check your answers. Ready?

A

Blue needs your help finding the letter **A**. **A** is the first letter of the alphabet. Circle every **A** you see. How many can you find? Use the decoder to check your answer.

B

This is the Big Bakery. Will you help Blue find the letter **B** here? Circle every **B**. How many did you find? Beautiful!

C

Now Blue is looking for the letter C. Will you underline every C in the dessert section? How many did you find?

DELICIOUS DESSERTS

D

Do you see the letter **D**?
Count and circle every **D**.
How many did you find?

E

Blue met Green Puppy at Goldie's Grocery.
Will you help them find more letters?
Great!

How many times do you see letter E in the bread aisle?
Underline them. Excellent letter finding!

F and G

Do you see the letter F? Circle every F then write how many you found.

Now draw a box around every letter G. How many did you find?

H

Blue met Periwinkle at the House of Hats! Hat begins with the letter H. Circle each H. Count how many you see.

I and J

Can you spy the letter I in Jerry's Ice Cream Parlor? Circle every I. How many did you find?

The letter J comes after I. Underline every J. How many do you see?

K

Look! Blue and her friends are at the park.
How many signs do you see that have the letter **K**?
Use the decoder to check your answer.

L

Now, help Blue find the letter **L**.
How many times do you see letter **L**?
Circle each **L**.

M

Here's Magenta at the Music Store. Maybe Blue will find the letter **M** here. Will you help her? Circle every **M**. How many did you find?

N

Do you see the letter **N**? Underline every **N** then write how many you found.

O

Oh, look! Blue is on a hunt for the letter **O**! Will you help her find the letter **O** in Olly's Sports Shop? Underline every **O** you see. How many did you find?

P

After O comes...P! Circle every P then write how many you found.

Q and R

Blue is looking for more letters at the library.
Find and circle the words that start with the letter Q.
How many did you find?

How many times do you see the letter R in the library?
Count them with Blue!

S The library is a super place to find the letter **S**. Underline every **S** then write how many you found.

T

The Toy Store is a terrific place to look for the letter T! Circle every T you see. How many did you find?

U

What comes after **T**? You got it! **U**! Will you help Blue look for the letter **U** along the sidewalk? Underline every **U** that you see. How many did you find? Good job!

V

Some of the plants in Wally's Greenhouse start with the letter V. Count and circle each V.

W

Blue also sees the letter W at the greenhouse. Circle every W then write how many you found.

X and Y

On her way home, Blue sees the letter **X**. Do you? Circle each **X** and write how many you found.

You can count each **Y**, too. How many do you see?

Z

The letter **Z** is the last letter in the alphabet. Will you help Blue find the letter **Z**? Great! Draw a box around every **Z**. How many did you find?

Blue skidooed back home. Now she wants to write down all the letters that you helped her find, from **A** to **Z**. Will you help her? If you sing the alphabet song, it will help you write them in order.

Way to go! Thanks for all your help.

Flashcards

Directions:

1. Tear out each flashcard page.

2. Cut the flashcards apart on the dotted lines

Review the letters with your child. Practice saying the letter sounds and singing the alphabet in order. Make up your own activities and games with the letter flashcards.

Flashcard Fun Activity Ideas

Finding Letters - Say a word that your child may already know and see if he/she can find the correct letter for the beginning sound of the word. Be sure to sound it out slowly and clearly. Or, your child can find the first letter in his or her own name. Variation - use names of characters from the Blues Clues stories or names of people in your house.

Letter Guess – Lay out several flashcards on the floor. Choose any letter and describe it to your child. See if he/she can guess the letter. For example, you might say, "I am thinking of a letter that is round on one side and open on the other. It is the letter that begins the word cookie and cat."

Letter Action - Choose a letter in the flashcard deck and have your child show an action that begins with that letter. For example, if the letter is M, your child could march in place or meow like a cat. Reverse - let your child show an action first and then help him/her to find the letter that starts the word by sounding out the words and emphasizing the letter sounds.

Beginning Spelling - Help your child spell different words with the flashcards. Start with simple two or three letter words of familiar objects like cat, bat, mop, dog, and sit. Help your child sound out the words by focusing on the sound of each letter.

Finding Hidden Letters – Choose a flashcard and encourage your child to see if he/she can find more of the same letter in your house. Encourage him or her to look in different places like on the refrigerator (or inside), on clothing, and on covers of books; give hints if your child is having a hard time getting started. Have your child race against the clock to see how many letters he/she can find in 4-5 minutes. Try beating the record the next time with a new letter.

Hidden Letter Pictures – Choose a letter from the flashcard deck and write that letter on a piece of paper. Encourage your child to make a picture from the letter. See if he/she can make a picture that starts with the same letter. For example, if the letter is B, try to make the picture look like a bear or a boat.

Flashcard Quiz – Have your child stand at the other side of the room and see if he/she can guess the letter on the card that you are holding up. If correct, your child can advance one step forward. See if your child can make it all the way across the room by identifying the letters correctly. Variation: Every time your child identifies a letter correctly, he/she gets a small token like a penny, a chip, a small candy, or a sticker.

G

J

F

I

E

H

M

P

L

O

K

N

S

R

U

Q

T

Z

W

Y

V

X

Aa Bb Cc Dd Ee Ff Gg Hh Ii Jj Kk Ll Mm Nn Oo Pp Qq Rr Ss Tt Uu Vv Ww Xx Yy Zz

Now Blue and her friends are practicing writing letters. Will you help them? Great!
Start by writing the capital letter **A**.

Let's write lowercase **a**.

Blue wants to practice capital B.
That's the first letter in Blue's name!

Write lowercase b, too!

Will you help Mr. Salt and Mrs. Pepper practice writing capital C? Yeah!

1 C 1 C C

Practice writing lowercase c.

1 c 1 c c

Now you can practice writing capital D.

1 2 D D D

Write lowercase d.

1 2 d d d

Magenta knows that E comes after D.
Practice writing the capital letter E.

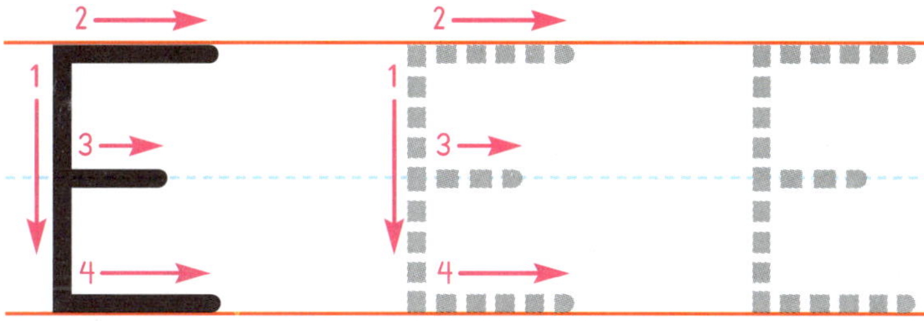

Don't forget lowercase e!

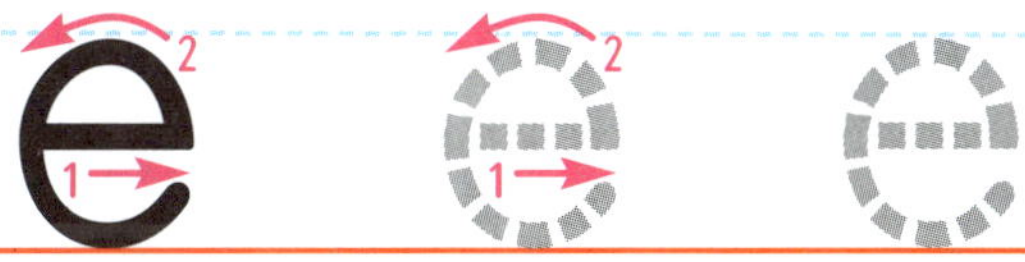

Aa Bb Cc Dd Ee **Ff** Gg Hh Ii Jj Kk Ll Mm Nn Oo Pp Qq Rr Ss Tt Uu Vv Ww Xx Yy Zz

Slippery already practiced writing capital F. Now it's your turn!

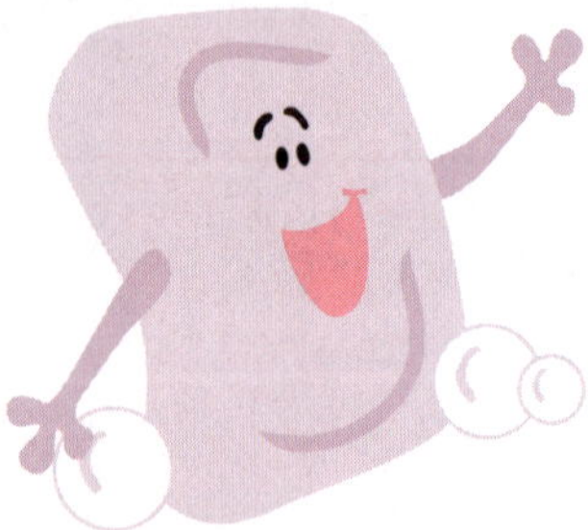

Practice writing lowercase f.

Aa Bb Cc Dd Ee Ff **Gg** Hh Ii Jj Kk Ll Mm Nn Oo Pp Qq Rr Ss Tt Uu Vv Ww Xx Yy Zz

Green Puppy's name starts with the capital letter **G**. Practice writing capital **G**.

G G G

Now write lowercase **g**.

g g g

Blue wants to write the capital letter H in the Handy Dandy Notebook. Will you write capital H with her?

Will you write lowercase h, too? Great!

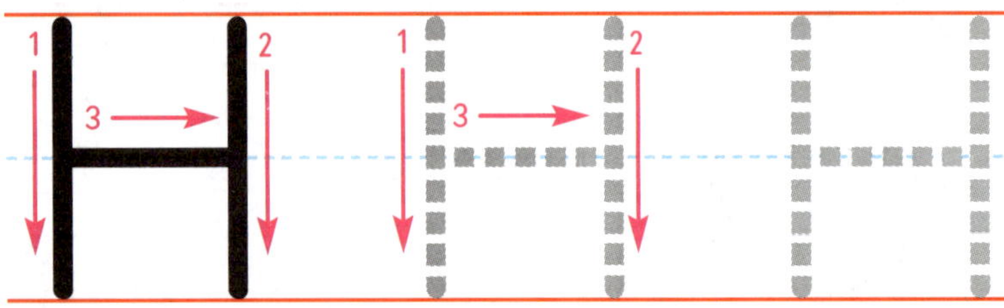

Now practice writing capital I.

Write lowercase i.

Aa Bb Cc Dd Ee Ff Gg Hh Ii **Jj** Kk Ll Mm Nn Oo Pp
Qq Rr Ss Tt Uu Vv Ww Xx Yy Zz

Blue knows that the letter J comes next! Write capital J.

J J J

Write lowercase j, too!

j j j

Help Purple Kangaroo write the capital letter K.

K K K

Practice writing lowercase k.

k k k

Look how the capital letter L goes down then across! Practice writing capital L.

Now write lowercase l.

Mailbox loves the letter M! It reminds him of Mail Time! Write capital M.

Let's write lowercase m.

Aa Bb Cc Dd Ee Ff Gg Hh Ii Jj Kk Ll Mm **Nn** Oo Pp Qq Rr Ss Tt Uu Vv Ww Xx Yy Zz

The letter N comes after M.
Practice writing capital N.

Will you write lowercase n, too? Great!

Orange Kitten already practiced writing capital O. Now it's your turn!

1 O

1

Practice writing lowercase o.

1 o

1

Help Periwinkle write capital P.

Write lowercase p, too!

Aa Bb Cc Dd Ee Ff Gg Hh Ii Jj Kk Ll Mm Nn Oo Pp
Qq Rr Ss Tt Uu Vv Ww Xx Yy Zz

The letter Q is next! Practice writing capital Q.

Q Q Q

Now write lowercase q.

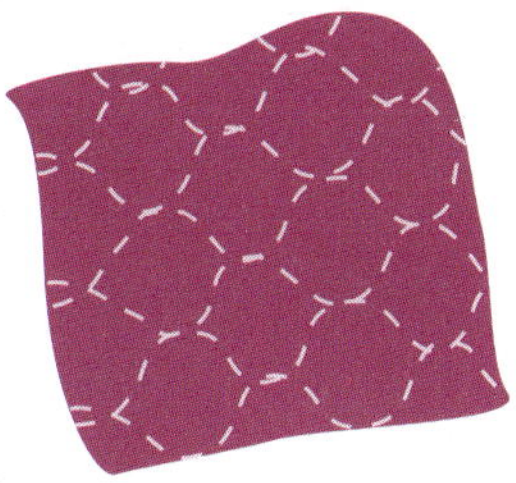

q q q

Do you know what letter Blue wants to practice now? R!
Help Blue write capital R.

R R R

Don't forget lowercase r!

r r r

Aa Bb Cc Dd Ee Ff Gg Hh Ii Jj Kk Ll Mm Nn Oo Pp
Qq Rr **Ss** Tt Uu Vv Ww Xx Yy Zz

Slippery loves the letter S because it's the first letter in his name. Practice writing capital S.

Practice writing lowercase s, too!

Tickety's name starts with the letter T. Write capital T.

T T T

Now write lowercase t.

t t t

Aa Bb Cc Dd Ee Ff Gg Hh Ii Jj Kk Ll Mm Nn Oo Pp
Qq Rr Ss Tt **Uu** Vv Ww Xx Yy Zz

Mr. Salt and Mrs. Pepper know that U comes next.
Write capital U.

U U U

Write lowercase u, too!

u u u

Help Green Puppy write capital V and lowercase v.

V V V

v v v

Will you help her write capital W and lowercase w, too? Great!

W W W

w w w

Aa Bb Cc Dd Ee Ff Gg Hh Ii Jj Kk Ll Mm Nn Oo Pp
Qq Rr Ss Tt Uu Vv Ww **Xx** Yy Zz

The letter X is next! Practice writing capital X.

Now write lowercase x!

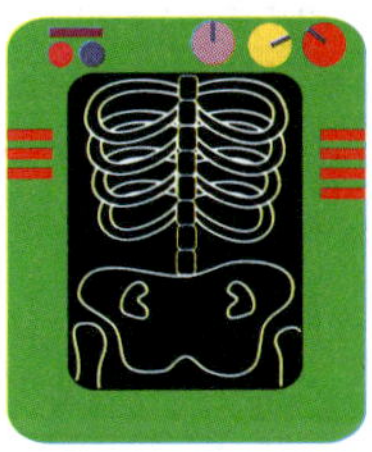

Blue is almost at the end of the alphabet. Will you help her write capital Y and lowercase y? Great!

Now write lowercase y!

Now help her write capital **Z**!

Z Z Z

Now write lowercase **z**!

z z z

Great job! Thanks for helping Blue and her friends practice their letters!

Beginning Letter Sounds

Decoder Workbook

Play along with Blue and:

- recognize beginning letter sounds
- identify partner letters

Reveals hidden answers!

Includes a SPECIAL DECODER!

Now Blue is collecting letter sounds in her sound machine. She's looking for words that begin with every letter of the alphabet. Can you help her? You'll need the special decoder included in this book. Use it to see the answers hidden next to Blue's pawprints.

Blue is looking for the Bb sound. She found some bunnies. Bunny begins with the Bb sound.

Practice saying Bb then help Blue add it to the sound machine by tracing Bb on the sound disk.

Do you see anything else that begins with the Bb sound? Circle the pictures and use your decoder to check your answers.

A buzzing bee begins with **Bb**. What other letters sounds can you find here? Say the name of each picture and circle the letter sound that it begins with.

Ll Mm

Uu Ii

Rr Dd

Aa Oo

Blue knows that every letter has two forms – capital and lowercase. And both forms of a letter have the same sound. Will you help Blue match the letters with the same sound? Draw a line from each capital letter to the matching lowercase letter.

B	m
I	r
A	b
R	i
M	a

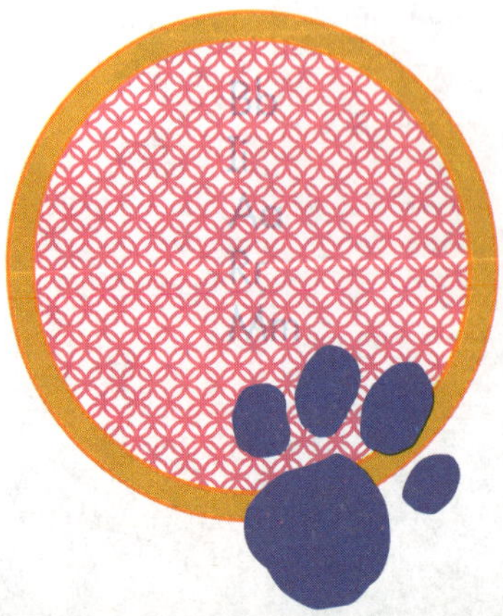

Blue is looking for something that starts with the Ww sound. Look, she found a wagon! Will you write Ww on Blue's sound disk? Wonderful!

Practice saying the Ww sound.

What other letter sounds can you help Blue find at the playground? Say the name of each picture and circle the letter sound that it begins with. Use your decoder to check your answers.

Wow, that's six more letters for Blue's sound machine!

Hey, Blue found something that starts with the Hh sound. Helmet! Blue always wears a helmet when she rides her scooter. Look, Periwinkle has a helmet on, too!

Practice saying the Hh sound and write Hh on the sound disk.

Blue found some more capital and lowercase letters to match. Will you help her? Color the block with the capital letter that is the partner of the lowercase letter in each row. Remember, matching capital and lowercase letters have the same sound.

d	B	D	R
n	N	W	M
h	R	J	H
k	W	K	A
j	L	S	J

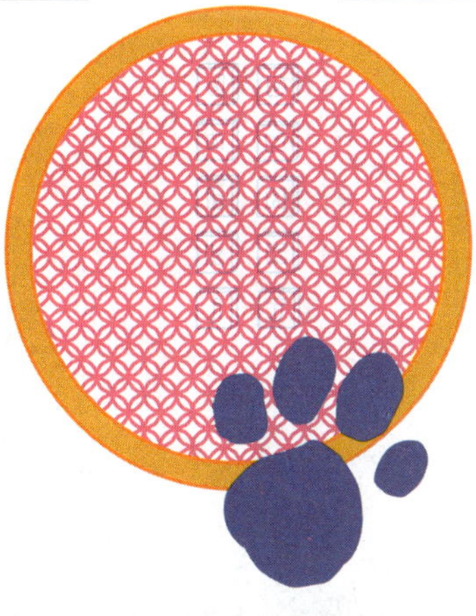

Blue is looking for things that begin with the Gg and Vv sounds. She found a garden – full of vegetables! Write Vv and Gg on different sound disks. Very good!

Help Blue find more letter sounds in the vegetable garden. Circle the vegetables that start with the Tt, Cc and Ll sounds. Color the friend whose name starts with the P sound. Look next to Blue's pawprints to see if you're right.

Uh oh, it's starting to rain. Blue found the perfect Uu sound that goes with rain. Umbrella!

Practice saying the Uu sound and write Uu on one of Blue's sound disks.

Blue found some pictures of things that begin with the same sounds as her friends' names. Will you help her match them? Draw a line from Blue's friends to the pictures that start with the same sound.

Blue made a rainy day picture that looks just like the weather outside. She drew a zigzag bolt of lightning for the Zz sound at the beginning of zigzag. Find and color the zigzag lightning bolt.

Do you see a picture that begins with the Qq sound?
Quick! Circle it.

Practice saying the Qq and Zz letter sounds.

Maybe you can help Blue find some more letter sounds in the kitchen. Use the letters on the refrigerator to fill in the beginning sound of each word. Circle the letters that you use.

_____ lives

Blue used the letters that were left on the refrigerator to make a word that begins with the Xx sound. It's x-ray! Write Xx on the sound disk. Excellent!

Practice saying the Xx sound.

Blue found some things in the kitchen that have the same letter sound. Will you help her sort them? Color the pictures that start with the same sound in each row.

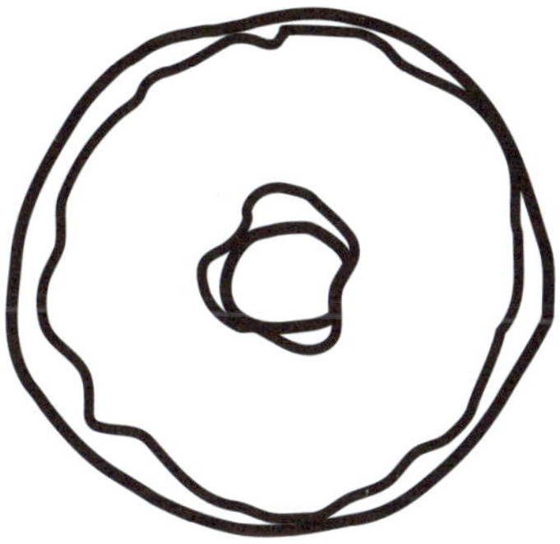
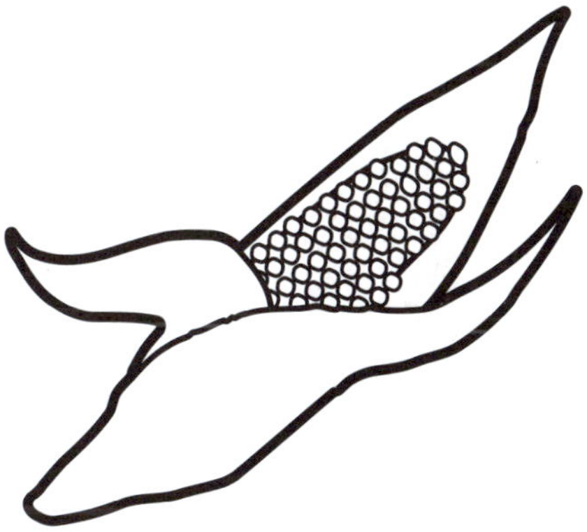

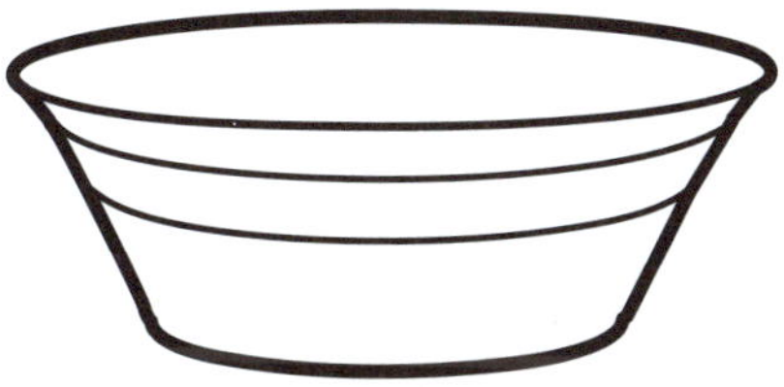
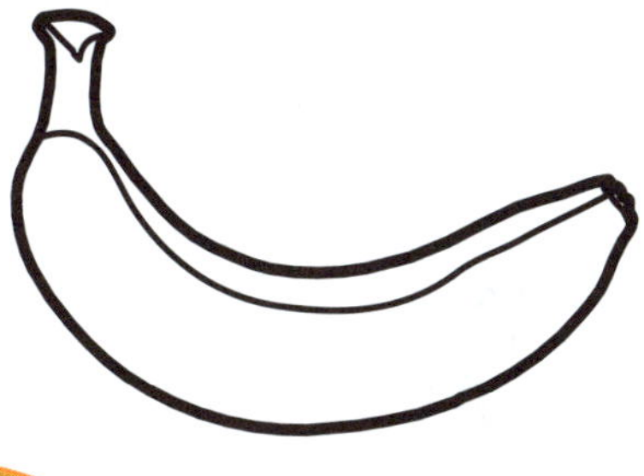

Blue's letter sound collection is all done. Now she wants to play it on her sound machine. Help her write the letters for all the sounds she found. Say the name of each picture and write the letter sound that it begins with.

Aa

  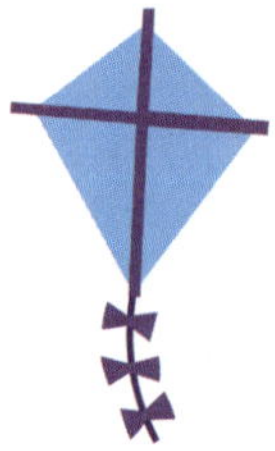  

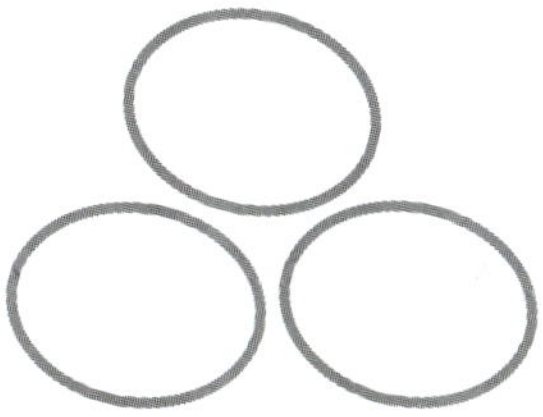   

 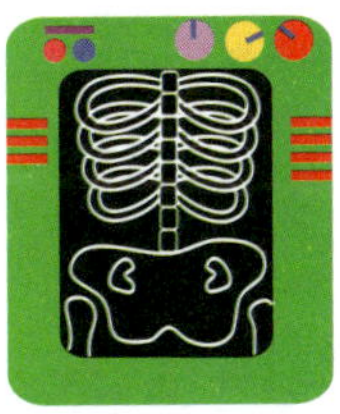  

Zz

Write the first letter of your name. Say the letter sound.

Draw three things that start with the same sound.

Reveals hidden answers!

Includes a SPECIAL DECODER!

Decoder Workbook

Word Families

Teach your child to:

- recognize common word endings
- identify rhyming sounds
- recognize short vowel sounds
- improve phonics and spelling skills

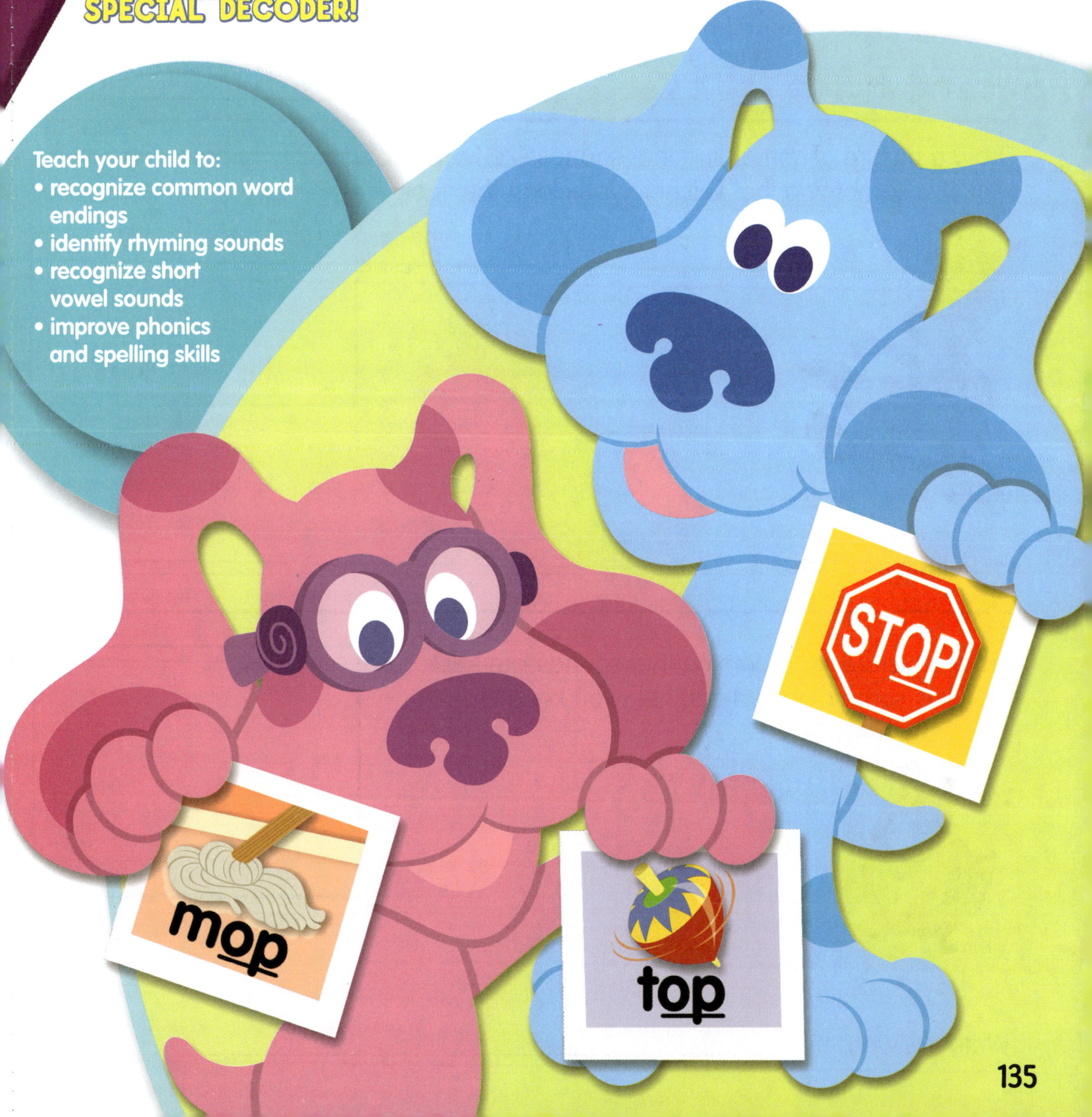

Draw a picture of something that sounds like c**at.**
Hint: Periwinkle has it on her head.

Write the word here.

Draw a picture of something that sounds like t**op.**
Hint: It is something that will help you clean the floor.

Write the word here.

Draw a picture of something that sounds like l**ock.**
Hint: It is something that can help you keep time.

Write the word here.

Blue and Magenta are making **word family** pictures for a school project. Will you help them make pictures for Miss Marigold's Word Family Wall?

You'll need the special decoder wand included in this book. Use it to see the answers hidden next to Blue's pawprints.

Blue and Magenta want to start with the **at** word family. Words in the **at** family rhyme with **pat**. Can you find three things whose names belong to the **at** family? Circle them.

Shhh! Periwinkle is taking a **nap**. **Nap** belongs to the **ap** word family. Will you help Magenta and Blue look for other things whose names belong to the **ap** word family? Circle two things that rhyme with **nap** and use the decoder to check your answers.

Look! Paprika and Cinnamon are playing with Blue's toy **van**. Blue wants pictures of other things whose names end in **an**.

Do you see three other things that belong to the **an** word family? Circle them. Use the decoder to check your answers.

Tickety can help sort the word family pictures Blue and Magenta have collected so far. Will you help too? Write the word family ending for each group of pictures.

ap at an

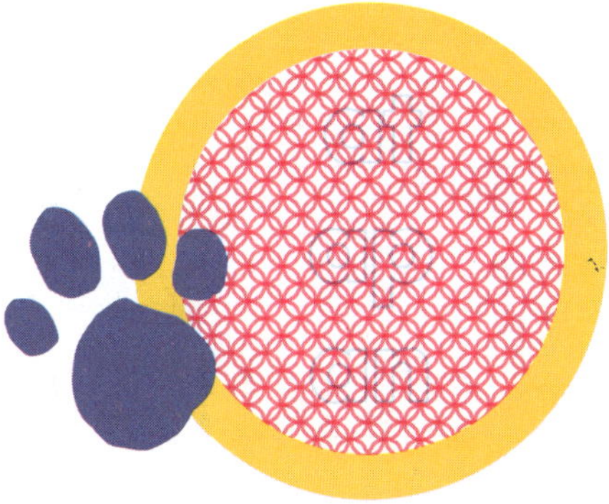

Now Blue and Magenta are trying to **spot** things that belong to the **ot** family. Words in the **ot** family rhyme with **spot**.

Do you **spot** three more things that end with the sound of **ot**? Circle them.

Hop! Hop! Hop! Purple Kangaroo is so excited! He is helping Blue and Magenta find things for the **op** word family photos! Words in the **op** family rhyme with **hop**.

Will you help him figure out which things to choose? Circle three things whose names end with **op**.

Magenta had a great idea! She wrote a rhyme about the **og** word family.

Read the rhyme and circle all the pictures of things whose names end with **og**.

 **and**  **went for a jog.**

They saw a little pink hog and a big pink  **.**

They passed a  **and saw a**  **.**

On top of the  **was a little green**  **.**

Pail and Shovel can help sort more pictures. Will you help, too? Say the name of each picture. Then draw a line to match the first letter in its name with the correct word family ending.

 **l** **op**

 **m** **og**

 **p** **op**

 **h** **ot**

 **t** **og**

Blue is cutting out pictures from magazines and circling the part that shows something whose name belongs to the **ip** word family. She circled the **tip** of the pencil. Say the name of everything you see in each picture. Circle three things whose names end in **ip**.

Magenta is cutting out pictures, too. She is circling things that belong to the **in** word family, like the pumpkin's big **grin**. Will you help Magenta? Say the name of everything you see in each picture. Circle three things whose names end in **in**.

Use the decoder to check your answers.

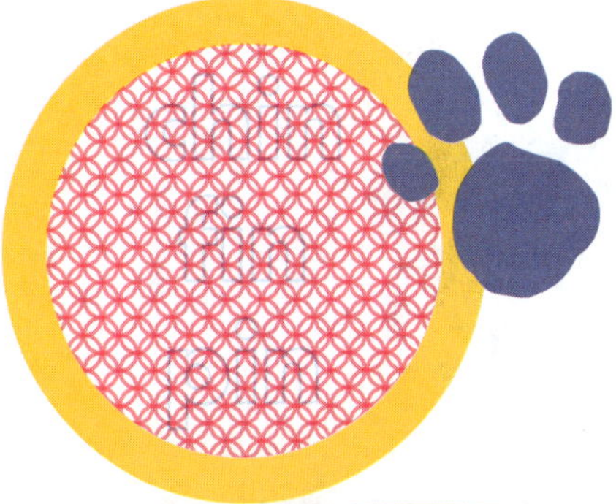

Blue is giving Green Puppy a great big **hug** because she found things for Blue's **ug** family pictures. **Hug** belongs to the **ug** word family.

Find and circle three things Green Puppy picked out for the **ug** word family picture.

Blue and Magenta asked their friends for help with the **um** word family pictures.

Find and circle two things whose names end in **um**. Then circle the friend who is doing something that ends in **um**.

Slippery Soap wants to sort these pictures for Blue and Magenta's project. Say the name of each picture. Then draw a line to match the first part of its name with the correct word family ending.

b - **ug**

sh **um**

dr **ug**

r **in**

p **ip**

Magenta and Blue are in the **den** looking for things for the **en** word family picture. **Den** belongs to the **en** word family.

Circle three things you see whose names end with **en**. Don't forget to use your decoder to check your answers!

Magenta wants to take an **ell** family photo. Periwinkle is helping her get ready. Will you help him by circling three things whose names end in **ell?**

Click! Magenta is taking **ick** word family photos! **Click** belongs to the **ick** word family.

Which two things should Magenta take pictures of? Circle them.

Tickety Tock is a clock, so Blue is drawing her friend for an **ock** word family picture. **Tock** and **clock** both end with the sound of **ock**.

What other things should Blue draw? Circle three things whose names belong to the **ock** word family.

Mr. Salt and Mrs. Pepper can help Blue and Magenta sort their pictures, but they need help remembering the word ending that goes with each picture.

Use the word endings in the box to finish writing the name of each object.

en	**ell**	**ick**	**ock**

br

b

p

s

Blue and Magenta have glued all their pictures onto poster paper. Now they have to put the correct word family name with each group of pictures. Circle the correct word family ending for each group.

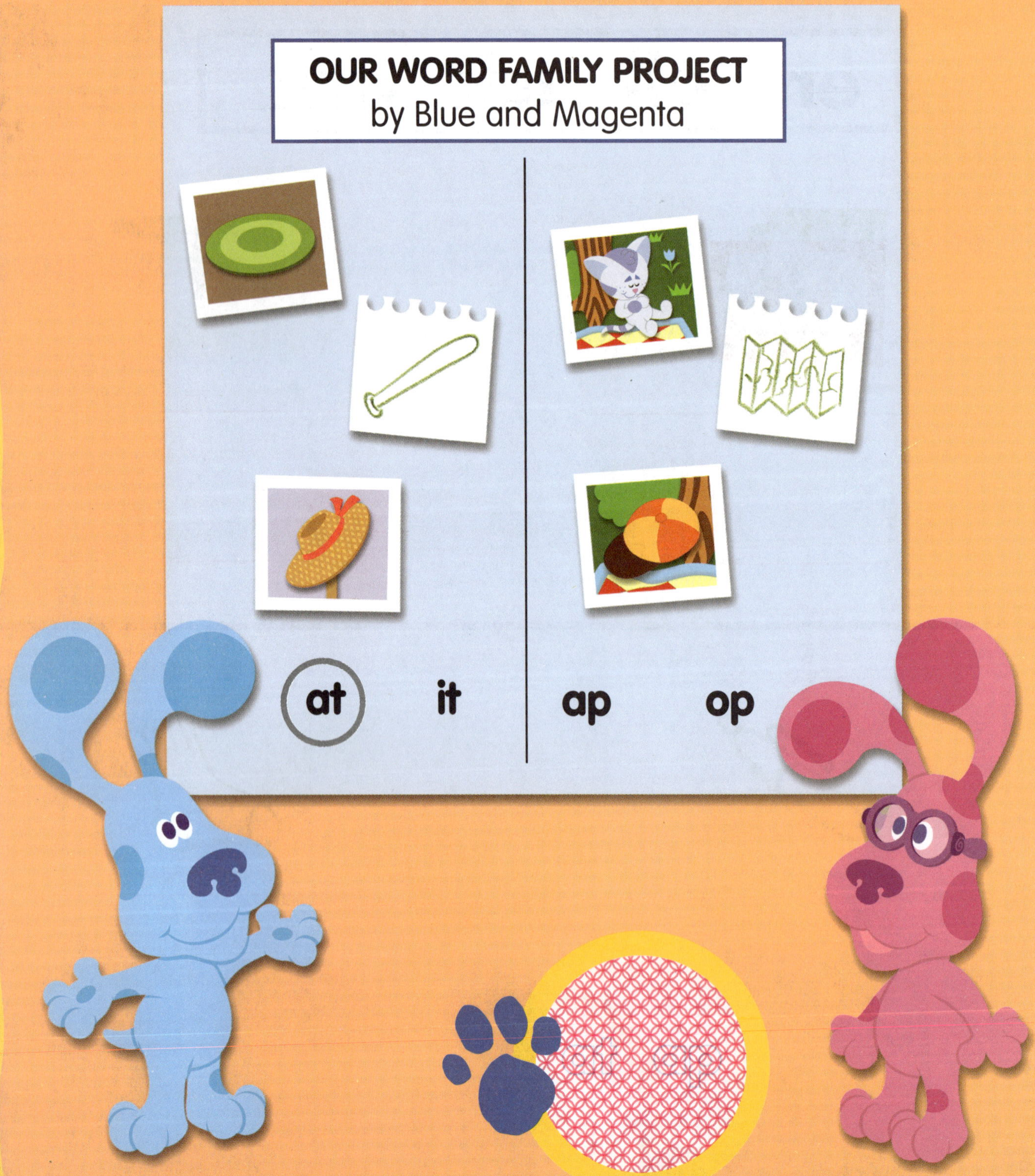

Circle the correct word family ending for each group of pictures.
Use your decoder to check your answers

in an

ot it

ap op

ug og

Circle the correct word family ending for each group of pictures.

ip op

an in

ug og

um ug

Circle the correct word family ending for each group of pictures.

en **in**

ell **en**

ock **ick**

ock **ick**

Look! Miss Marigold's Word Family Wall is almost finished. But a few of the pictures fell off their posters. Will you draw a line from each picture to the place where it belongs?

Great job! Thanks for all your help.